Wieners GONE WILD!

OUT-OF-THE-BALLPARK RECIPES
FOR EXTRAORDINARY HOT DOGS

Holly Schmidt & Allan Penn

Running Press
PHILADELPHIA · LONDON

© 2014 by Holly Schmidt and Allan Penn
Photography © 2014 by Hollan Publishing, Inc.
A Hollan Publishing, Inc. Concept

Published by Running Press,
A Member of the Perseus Books Group

Books published by Running Press are available at special discounts for bulk purchases in the United States by corporations, institutions, and other organizations. For more information, please contact the Special Markets Department at the Perseus Books Group, 2300 Chestnut Street, Suite 200, Philadelphia, PA 19103, or call (800) 810-4145, ext. 5000, or e-mail special.markets@perseusbooks.com.

ISBN 978-0-7624-4727-5
Library of Congress Control Number: 2013945766

E-book ISBN 978-0-7624-5177-7

9   8   7   6   5   4   3   2   1
Digit on the right indicates the number of this printing

Cover and interior design by Jason Kayser
Edited by Jordana Tusman
Typography: Museo and House Script

Running Press Book Publishers
2300 Chestnut Street
Philadelphia, PA 19103-4371

Visit us on the web!
www.offthemenublog.com

To Caleb, Owen, Griffin, Charlotte, Nick, and Jax—
like everything we do, this book is dedicated
to you. Each one of you eats hot dogs like a boss.

CONTENTS

About

HOT DOGS
&
SAUSAGES

EVERYONE LOVES HOT DOGS. *EVERYONE.* When we told people we were writing a hot dog cookbook, without exception we heard, "I love hot dogs!" This book is a collection of over-the-top recipes for America's favorite food. Some are easy and quick to put together, others are more labor-intensive (but worth it!)—and we're pretty sure most of them haven't been done before. We hope you dazzle your friends with your wiener creations and have as much fun making them as we have.

THE MIRACLE THAT IS THE TUBE STEAK

As we were developing the recipes, we learned something that surprised us: Hot dogs, while delicious on their own, are the perfect foil for a wide variety of foods, from fried clams to Caesar salad to quesadillas. Turns out, the smoky, salty flavor and juicy, greasy snap of a hot dog serves to enhance almost anything it touches, in much the same way bacon improves dishes from Brussels sprouts to braised chicken. Rather than competing with the sophisticated flavors we threw at them, hot dogs rose to the occasion and made them better, whether it was the peppercorns and brandy cream sauce of Wiener au Poivre (page 99), or the delicious apples and thyme of the Apple Pie Dog (page 81).

THE HISTORY OF THE HOT DOG

The hot dog was born in Frankfurt, Germany, sometime around the 13th century, where they were served at imperial coronations. (See, we *knew* hot dogs were the food of kings!) Nobody is sure how or when they made their way to America, but it appears to have been sometime in the late 1800s. They quickly became a popular staple at baseball games and fairs, because they were easy to eat, inexpensive, and totally delicious. The positive association most people have with hot dogs and baseball games, carnivals, and backyard barbecues only serves to solidify and heighten their exalted place in our culinary culture. Everybody has a happy hot dog memory.

WHAT IS A HOT DOG?

Hot dogs are traditionally made from pork and/or beef, spices like garlic and paprika, salt, and preservatives like sodium nitrite. The meat mixture is put into casings (natural casings, which are sheep intestines—yes—or synthetic casings that are removed after cooking to make "skinless" dogs) and cooked. When you buy them at the grocery store, they are actually ready to eat, but most people prefer to cook them again before eating, to heat them up and caramelize the exterior. Hot dogs taste good no matter how you cook them, and we leave that up to you in our recipes. Want to grill the dog? Awesome. Prefer to throw it in a pan on the stove? Fantastic. Whatever makes your skirt fly up is fine by us.

TYPES OF HOT DOGS

Today, there are many different kinds of hot dogs on the market, and much regional variation. A lot of hot dogs are made by local, often family-owned businesses, and flavors and styles can vary widely from state to state. Here in New England, Kayem Foods,

Inc. (maker of Fenway Franks) dogs reign supreme, and in New York, many of the most-loved hot dogs are made by Marathon Enterprises, Inc., owner of Sabrett. In Chicago, the famous Chicago dog is an all-beef, natural casing hot dog. Your local grocery store probably sells a few different local brands of natural-casing and skinless franks, as well as the big national brands like Oscar Mayer, Ball Park, and Boar's Head.

Hot dog preference is truly subjective; if you don't already have a favorite, we recommend you try a few different kinds until you find one that you really love. Our recipes will work with any kind of dog, so use your own judgment about skinless versus natural casing. Sometimes you want the snap of the natural casing, and sometimes you don't.

Any of the recipes in this cookbook can be made with a turkey dog or a veggie dog, too—we don't roll that way, but you can if you want to!

The recipes in *Wieners Gone Wild!* are all our own creations, cooked up in our studio in Gloucester, Massachusetts, over many months of experimentation. We intentionally excluded classic regional specialties like the Chicago dog, because recipes for those are readily available in a lot of other places. We wanted this book to be a collection of unique hot dog wonders, or at least new twists on old favorites, and we hope we've succeeded.

But to satisfy your curiosity, the following is a quick rundown of how America likes its famous dogs:

CHICAGO DOG: An all-beef hot dog served in a steamed poppy seed bun and blanketed with chopped raw onions, sweet pickle relish, sport peppers (small, green, medium-hot pickled peppers), a pickle spear, tomatoes, yellow mustard, and a sprinkle of celery salt. These are religion in Chicago, but you can sometimes find them outside the Windy City as well.

SLAW DOG: Popular in the South, a slaw dog is topped with a creamy coleslaw that may or may not include chili or barbecue sauce.

RED DOG: As far as we know, you can only find these neon-red dogs in Maine, where they are also known as "red snappers," due to their natural casings that snap when you bite into them. The color doesn't affect the taste, and kids love it.

KOSHER DOG: Popular in New York and New Jersey, kosher dogs are all-beef and usually topped with sauerkraut and smeared with mustard.

CHILI DOG: Out West, people like their all-beef hot dogs topped with meat chili, chopped onions, and usually shredded cheddar.

HOT BUNS!

Here at WGW world headquarters, we love a homemade bun—whether it's a standard yeast roll, a fresh, buttery biscuit, a slab of cornbread, a crisp popover, or a twist of home-made pretzel—you just can't beat bread you make yourself. That said, more often than not, we're throwing our wieners onto store-bought rolls, what with the demands of work and family. So we're giving you our recipes for homemade buns for those times when you really want to crank up the mojo on your wiener-making, but our recipes all have store-bought bun options, too.

A NOTE ABOUT THE RECIPES

We lean toward homemade, in every case: homemade ketchup, homemade mac and cheese, homemade salsa. We lean that way because it all tastes about a hundred times better than the stuff you buy at the store, and we like to cook. But if you don't care, or if you don't have the time to cook everything from scratch, we've noted store-bought substitutions where appropriate. One thing we do *not* condone is boxed mixes for baked goods. It is just as easy to mix your own flour, sugar, baking powder, and salt as it is to buy a box—and it tastes better and costs less. If you'd rather use Jiffy cornbread mix than make the unbelievably delicious—and stone simple—recipe provided, that's your choice. But we hope you'll try it our way, at least some of the time.

AND, YOU'RE OFF!

As we leave you to embark on your *Wieners Gone Wild!* adventures, we hope you discover that, while a simple hot dog with mustard is pretty good, the almighty wiener deserves to go wild every now and then. Have fun!

NOTE: *Each hot dog recipe and sub-recipe for toppings and sauces in this book makes enough for eight dogs, unless noted otherwise.*

Homemade
CONDIMENTS
& BUNS

Hot Dog Buns

Is there anything better than homemade bread? No, there isn't. Unless it's homemade bread with a hot dog in it! This recipe, inspired by one from King Arthur Flour, makes a tender, soft white sandwich bread. Keep in mind that you might need more or less flour depending on the day's levels of humidity. Pay attention to the texture of the dough; it should be pretty relaxed and moist, rather than stiff and dry, to ensure tender buns. Use just enough flour to keep the dough from sticking to your hands and the counter as you knead it.

· · ◆ ◆ ◆ ◆ · ·

Dissolve the sugar and yeast in the warm water. Add the milk, oil, salt, and flour. (We use a stand mixer to mix the dough, starting with the paddle attachment and switching to the dough hook attachment for the kneading. You can also use a food processor or do it all by hand the old-school way.) Mix the dough until it comes together in a slightly sticky ball, adding more flour a little at a time if it's too sticky. Switch to the dough hook (if you're using a stand mixer) or turn the dough out onto a floured work surface (if you're

(recipe continues)

MAKES 18 BUNS

2 tablespoons granulated sugar

2 tablespoons active dry yeast

½ cup warm water

2 cups warm milk (whole or 2% is best)

2 tablespoons vegetable oil, plus more as needed

2 teaspoons salt

6 cups all-purpose flour

1 large egg

kneading by hand). Knead the dough until it is smooth and elastic. This will take about 5 minutes in a food processor, 8 to 10 minutes in a stand mixer, and about 10 minutes by hand.

Put the dough into a greased bowl and turn it to coat the entire ball with oil. Cover the bowl with plastic wrap and put it in a warm place to rise. Let the dough rise until doubled, about 1½ hours.

Turn the dough out onto a lightly oiled work surface. Divide the dough into 18 equal pieces. Shape each piece into a ball, then into a cylinder about 4½ inches in length. Flatten each cylinder in the middle slightly so when it rises it will be gently rounded. Place the cylinders ½ inch apart on a greased baking sheet. (They'll grow together when they rise, making the classic New England–style soft sides that are so wonderful when buttered and grilled.) We have a special hot dog roll pan that our friends sent us from the King Arthur Flour catalog—you don't need it, but it makes perfect New England–style rolls every time. If you don't want New England–style rolls, place them 3 inches apart so they will brown all over.

Cover the baking sheet with a clean dish towel and let the dough rise in a warm place until almost doubled, about 45 minutes.

Preheat the oven to 400°F.

Beat the egg with 1 tablespoon of cold water and brush the buns with the egg wash. Bake the buns for 20 minutes or until they are light brown. Place the buns on a wire rack to cool.

Buns are best on the day they're baked, but they can be stored in an airtight container for up to 2 days or frozen for up to 1 month.

Buttermilk Biscuit Buns

These are classic, fluffy Southern biscuits, perfect for the Soul Dog (page 93) or any wiener with a good sauce that deserves to be mopped up. It's really important that the butter and buttermilk are cold, since it's the steam created by the melting butter in the oven that creates the desirable layered texture in a good biscuit. Biscuits are among the easiest breads to make—they come together in about twenty minutes total—so they are a cinch to make at a moment's notice.

Preheat the oven to 450°F.

Whisk together the flour, baking powder, baking soda, sugar, and salt in the bowl of a food processor (or a mixing bowl if you're doing it by hand).

Add the butter and pulse quickly (or cut it by hand into the flour mixture with two knives or a pastry blender) until the mixture resembles coarse meal. Add the buttermilk and process until the dough gathers in moist clumps, about 10 quick pulses. If you're

(recipe continues)

MAKES 8 BUNS

4 cups all-purpose flour

4 teaspoons baking powder

1 teaspoon baking soda

2 teaspoons granulated sugar

1 teaspoon salt

8 ounces (2 sticks) cold unsalted butter, cut into 8 pieces

1½ cups plus 2 tablespoons cold buttermilk

mixing by hand, stir the mixture with a rubber spatula until the mixture forms a moist, sticky dough.

Transfer the dough to a lightly floured surface and pat it into an 8 x 12-inch rectangle. Cut the dough into 8 even rectangles with a sharp knife and place them on an ungreased cookie sheet. Bake until the biscuits are light brown on top, about 10 to 12 minutes. Serve immediately. Biscuits are best eaten within a few hours of baking, but they can be stored in an airtight container for up to 1 day.

Popovers

MAKES 12 POPOVERS

**4 large eggs, warmed
(still in their shells)
in a cup of hot water for
10 minutes**

1½ cups warm whole milk

½ teaspoon salt

1½ cups all-purpose flour

**3 tablespoons unsalted
butter, melted**

The popover is a little culinary miracle—a simple batter of eggs, melted butter, milk, flour, and salt goes into the oven and puffs up into a crisp wonder with a soft interior that is delicious on its own and a marvel when paired with savory fillings. You can even dip the tops in melted butter and cinnamon-sugar for a fantastic breakfast treat.

· · ◆ ◆ ◆ ◆ · ·

Move the oven rack to the lowest position and preheat the oven to 450°F. Grease a 12-cup muffin tin, both inside the cups and between them. (The popovers "pop" over the top and will stick to the part of the muffin tin between the cups if you don't grease them.)

In a large bowl, whisk together the eggs, milk, and salt. Add the flour all at once and whisk until smooth. Whisk in the melted butter.

Pour the batter into the muffin cups (each cup should be three-quarters full). Bake the popovers for 20 minutes without opening the oven door. Reduce the heat to 350°F and bake for an additional 10 to 15 minutes, or until the popovers are a deep, golden brown. Remove the popovers from the oven and pierce the top of each one with a sharp paring knife to release the steam. Serve immediately.

Cornbread

This cornbread recipe is inspired by *Cook's Illustrated*, and it's worth taking the time to make it from scratch. You can use store-bought cornbread (or a box mix, which we wholeheartedly do *not* recommend) if you want, but we think homemade, in this case, is far superior.

Preheat the oven to 400°F. Grease a 9 x 13-inch rectangular baking pan.

Whisk together the flour, cornmeal, baking powder, baking soda, and salt in a medium bowl until combined. In a food processor or blender, process the brown sugar, thawed corn kernels, and buttermilk until combined, about 5 seconds. Add the eggs and process until well combined (corn lumps will remain), about 5 more seconds.

Using a rubber spatula, make a well in the center of the dry ingredients. Pour the wet ingredients into the well. Begin folding the dry ingredients into the wet, giving the mixture only a few turns to barely combine. Add the melted butter and continue folding until the dry ingredients are just moistened.

(recipe continues)

3 cups all-purpose flour

2 cups yellow cornmeal

4 teaspoons baking powder

½ teaspoon baking soda

1½ teaspoons salt

⅔ cup packed light brown sugar

1½ cups frozen corn kernels, thawed

2 cups buttermilk

4 large eggs

8 ounces (2 sticks) unsalted butter, melted and cooled slightly

Pour the batter into the prepared baking dish and smooth the surface with the rubber spatula. Bake until the cornbread is golden brown and a toothpick inserted into the center comes out clean, 25 to 35 minutes. Cool until just warm before cutting into 8 rectangles and serving. Store well-wrapped with plastic wrap for up to 2 days.

"A hot dog at the ballgame beats roast beef at the Ritz."

—Humphrey Bogart

Ketchup

Once you taste this, you will never go back to Heinz. We swear. You can use fresh tomatoes if it's August and you're near a farm stand—otherwise, canned are better than the winter tomatoes you buy at the supermarket. Canned tomatoes are actual vine-ripened fresh tomatoes, so they have superior flavor, and the texture is irrelevant because you're cooking them anyway.

MAKES 3 CUPS

1 bay leaf

1 cinnamon stick

4 whole cloves

¼ teaspoon whole allspice berries, approximately 5 to 8 depending on size

¼ teaspoon red pepper flakes

¼ teaspoon celery seeds

1 (28-ounce) can whole peeled tomatoes (imported Italian ones are best)

1 medium yellow onion, chopped

1 dried chile de árbol pepper

1 garlic clove, minced

½ cup cider vinegar

1½ teaspoons kosher salt

5 tablespoons packed dark brown sugar

Freshly ground black pepper

(recipe continues)

23

Wrap the bay leaf, cinnamon, cloves, allspice, red pepper flakes, and celery seeds in a double layer of cheesecloth and tie it into a bundle with kitchen twine.

Place the tomatoes, onion, chile, garlic, vinegar, salt, and brown sugar in a medium saucepan, and season to taste with black pepper. Add the spice bundle and cook over medium heat, stirring frequently, until the onions are very soft, approximately 45 minutes.

Remove the spice bundle from the pan and puree the sauce with an immersion blender or (very carefully!) in the blender. Strain the sauce through a fine-mesh sieve into a clean saucepan.

Put the sauce back on the stove over medium-low heat. Cook, stirring occasionally, until the sauce is thickened, about 30 minutes.

Pour the ketchup into a Mason jar or other tightly sealed container and store it in the refrigerator for up to 3 weeks.

Barbecue Sauce

MAKES 2 CUPS

1 cup ketchup

¼ cup white vinegar

¼ cup packed dark brown sugar

2 tablespoons paprika

1 tablespoon olive oil

1 tablespoon chili powder

½ teaspoon to 1 teaspoon cayenne pepper (depending on how spicy you like it)

2 garlic cloves, minced

You can certainly use store-bought barbecue sauce, but when it's this easy to make from scratch, you may never have to. This is a thick, slightly sweet, spicy sauce, great on ribs or chicken as well as hot dogs.

· · ✦ · ✦ ◆ ✦ · ✦ · ·

Mix all ingredients together in a saucepan with ¼ cup of water. Bring the mixture to a simmer over medium-high heat. Reduce the heat and simmer for 15 minutes, until the sauce thickens.

Traditional Spicy Mustard

MAKES ABOUT ⅔ CUP

½ cup cider vinegar

¼ cup mustard powder

3 tablespoons mustard seeds, ground in a blender or spice mill

3 teaspoons light brown sugar

1 teaspoon kosher salt

½ teaspoon turmeric

¼ teaspoon paprika

¼ teaspoon garlic powder

¼ teaspoon freshly ground black pepper

This is a spicy, grainy mustard with a real kick. It's very quick and easy to make, but you have to let it mellow in the fridge for a few days—ideally, a week—or it will be really bitter. If you want to eat it right away, you're better off using a high-quality store-bought mustard.

· · ✦ ◆ ✦ · ·

In a small saucepan, whisk together all of the ingredients and ½ cup of water to blend. Simmer the mixture over medium heat for 5 to 6 minutes or until the desired consistency is reached. Store the mustard in a Mason jar or other tightly sealed container in the refrigerator for at least 3 days and up to 1 month.

IRISH WHISKEY MUSTARD

· · ✦ ✦ ✦ · ·

½ cup Dijon mustard

1 tablespoon Irish whiskey

Stir the mustard and whiskey together in a small saucepan and simmer the mixture over medium-low heat for 5 minutes.

HONEY MUSTARD

· · ✦ ✦ ✦ · ·

½ cup Dijon mustard

1½ tablespoons honey

Stir the mustard and honey together in a small bowl.

BOURBON-BROWN SUGAR MUSTARD

· · ✦ ✦ ✦ · ·

½ cup Dijon mustard

1 tablespoon bourbon

2 tablespoons packed dark brown sugar

Stir the mustard, bourbon, and brown sugar together in a small saucepan and simmer the mixture over medium-low heat for 5 minutes.

SLUM DOGS

Down 'n' Dirty Wieners

Porked

You can thank us now: This is pulled pork and macaroni and cheese on a hot dog! And there is not a carnivore on the planet who will be able to resist it. We've included delicious homemade recipes for both—you can freeze any leftovers for emergency cravings—but if you don't have the time, you can use store-bought pulled pork and mac and cheese, which makes this dog a cinch to throw together.

· · ◆ ◆ ◆ ◆ ◆ · · ·

Place a hot dog in each bun and top it with hot pulled pork and macaroni and cheese. Serve with extra barbecue sauce on the side.

Makes about 12 cups of pulled pork. (You can freeze the leftovers for up to 2 months.)

8 grilled hot dogs

8 buttered, toasted hot dog buns (page 15 or store-bought)

2 cups barbecued pulled pork (recipe follows or store-bought)

2 cups macaroni and cheese (recipe follows or store-bought)

Barbecue Sauce (page 26 or store-bought)

3 tablespoons paprika

1 tablespoon
garlic powder

1 tablespoon mustard
powder

1 tablespoon packed
dark brown sugar

3 tablespoon coarse sea
salt or kosher salt

1 (5 to 7-pound) pork
shoulder roast

2 cups Barbecue Sauce
(page 26 or store-bought)

BARBECUED PULLED PORK

MAKES 6 TO 8 SERVINGS
or enough for 8 Porked Dogs with leftovers

In a small bowl, whisk together the paprika, garlic powder, mustard powder, brown sugar, and salt; rub the mixture all over the pork. Cover the pork with plastic wrap and refrigerate it for at least 1 hour or overnight.

Preheat the oven to 300°F.

Put the pork in a roasting pan and roast it for about 6 hours. An instant-read thermometer stuck into the thickest part of the pork should register 170°F, but essentially you just want to roast it until it's falling apart.

Take the meat out of the oven and let it sit for 20 minutes. While it's still warm, "pull" the meat into shreds with two forks. Put the shredded pork in a bowl and mix it with the barbecue sauce.

STOVETOP MACARONI & CHEESE

MAKES 4 SERVINGS
or enough for 8 Porked Dogs

8 ounces (about 1 cup) elbow macaroni

1 tablespoon unsalted butter

1 large egg, beaten

6 ounces evaporated milk

1 teaspoon mustard powder

1/4 teaspoon cayenne pepper

Hot sauce

Salt and freshly ground black pepper

2 cups freshly grated cheddar cheese

This recipe is inspired by one found in *The Best Recipe*, by the editors of *Cook's Illustrated*. It's a great book of the classic American recipes that all home cooks should have in their repertoires, and this simple stir-and-serve mac and cheese is no exception.

Boil the pasta according to its package directions, but reduce the cooking time by 1 minute. Drain and pour the pasta back into the cooking pot.

Over medium-low heat, add the butter and stir until it is completely melted.

In a small bowl, mix together the egg, milk, mustard powder, cayenne pepper, and hot sauce to taste; pour the mixture over the pasta. Stir until the sauce begins to thicken, about 3 to 5 minutes. Season to taste with salt and pepper.

Remove the pan from the heat, and then add the cheese in four installments, making sure the first is melted completely before adding the next. Serve immediately.

Barkin' Breakfast

You eat bacon and sausage for breakfast, right? Well, a hot dog is a sausage, so why shouldn't it make a regular appearance on your breakfast table? These adorable hash brown–crusted quiches are elegant enough to serve to guests for brunch, but they are equally at home on a SpongeBob plate in front of Saturday morning TV.

· · + ◆ ◆ ◆ + · ·

Preheat the oven to 450°F. Grease a 12-cup muffin tin. (Nonstick is best, as the potatoes tend to stick to a regular muffin tin. You can also use glass custard cups for a more refined presentation.)

Divide the hash browns evenly among the muffin tin cups. Using your fingers, press the potatoes against the sides and bottoms of the cups, forming a crust about ⅓ inch thick. Season the potatoes with salt and pepper to taste. Bake the crusts for 20 minutes or until they are browned on the edges.

While the hash browns are baking, beat the eggs in a bowl with the milk and season the mixture with salt and pepper. When the

(recipe continues)

MAKES 12 SERVINGS AS A SIDE DISH (ONE PER PERSON) OR 6 AS A MAIN COURSE (TWO PER PERSON)

1 (20-ounce) bag shredded hash browns, thawed if frozen

Salt and freshly ground black pepper

10 large eggs

½ cup milk (whole or 2%)

4 hot dogs, chopped

½ cup chopped fresh chives

12 bacon slices, cooked

3 cups shredded sharp cheddar cheese

hash browns have baked for 20 minutes, remove the muffin tin from the oven and lower the temperature to 375°F.

Evenly divide the hot dogs, chives, and bacon among the muffin tins. Pour the egg mixture into the muffin tins, evenly dividing it among the cups. Top each muffin tin cup with ¼ cup of cheese. Return the muffin tin to the oven and bake for 30 minutes or until the egg is set and the cheese is melted and browned. Serve immediately.

> *"It is a noble thing to make a damn good hot dog."*
>
> **—Anthony Bourdain**

Drunk Dog

If you like booze, this is the wiener for you. A hot dog is dipped in beer batter and deep-fried, then topped with a roasted tomatillo-tequila salsa. Don't worry about these affecting your ability to operate machinery, though—the alcohol cooks off, leaving the flavor of the beer and tequila behind. We can't speak for the margaritas you drink with them, however.

Whisk the egg in a bowl, and add the flour, beer, salt, and paprika. Whisk the batter until smooth.

Heat the oil in a large, deep pot or deep fryer to 375°F. (You must have a frying thermometer for this—you can buy one at any grocery store.) Dip the hot dogs one at a time into the beer batter and place them in the oil. Cook until the batter is crisp and browned, about 4 minutes. Transfer the fried hot dogs to a paper towel–lined plate.

When all the dogs are cooked, place them in the buns and top each with ½ cup of the salsa. (The frying oil can be saved and reused. Just strain it and put it in the refrigerator in an airtight container for up to 1 month.)

1 large egg

1 cup all-purpose flour

1 cup beer (any kind is fine)

¼ teaspoon salt

¼ teaspoon paprika

4 cups peanut or vegetable oil

8 hot dogs

8 hot dog buns (page 15 or store-bought)

2 cups Tequila-Lime Tomatillo Salsa (recipe follows)

TEQUILA-LIME TOMATILLO SALSA

MAKES ABOUT 3 CUPS

Preheat the oven to 450°F.

Toss the tomatillos, oil, salt, and ¼ teaspoon of the pepper together in a heavy roasting pan. Roast for 25 minutes, or until the tomatillos are soft and brown. Remove the tomatillos from the pan and place them on a cutting board to cool.

Place the roasting pan over two burners on high heat. Pour in the tequila and use a wooden spoon to stir up any brown bits from the bottom of the pan. Bring the tequila to a boil and cook for 1 minute to burn off the alcohol, and then pour it into a large bowl.

When the tomatillos are cool enough to handle, coarsely chop them and place them in the bowl with the tequila. Add the onion, tomatoes, jalapeño, garlic, cumin, cayenne, lime juice, and the remaining ¼ teaspoon of black pepper, and stir to combine.

6 tomatillos, peeled, seeded, and halved

2 tablespoons olive oil

½ teaspoon coarse sea salt or kosher salt

½ teaspoon freshly ground black pepper, divided

⅛ cup tequila

1 small red onion, chopped

2 large tomatoes, chopped

1 jalapeño pepper, finely chopped (with seeds)

3 garlic cloves, minced

¼ teaspoon ground cumin

¼ teaspoon cayenne pepper

Juice from 1½ limes (about 3 tablespoons)

Hushed Puppy

½ cup all-purpose flour

½ cup cornmeal

½ teaspoon salt

¼ teaspoon baking soda

½ teaspoon freshly ground black pepper

1 large egg

½ cup buttermilk

¼ cup minced onion (from about ¼ of a small onion)

4 cups peanut or vegetable oil

8 hot dogs

8 hot dog buns (page 15 or store-bought)

2 cups Collard Green Relish (recipe follows)

Hush puppies are a staple at fish fries all over the South, y'all, and for good reason—the little balls of fried cornmeal batter are crunchy and delicious. Here, we dip hot dogs into hush puppy batter, fry them up, and cover them with a blanket of spicy-sweet collard green relish, which is the perfect foil for the salty, smoky meat.

· · · ◆ ◆ ◆ · · ·

In a large bowl, whisk together the flour, cornmeal, salt, baking soda, and pepper. Add the egg and buttermilk and stir until just combined. Add the onion. Heat the oil in a large, deep pot to 375°F. (You must have a frying thermometer for this. You can buy one at any grocery store.) Dip the hot dogs in the batter and place them in the oil, two at a time. Cook the dogs until the batter is brown and crisp, about 4 to 5 minutes. Transfer the fried hot dogs to a paper towel–lined plate and repeat with the remaining dogs. Place the hot dogs in the buns and top each with ¼ cup of relish.

COLLARD GREEN RELISH

MAKES ABOUT 3 CUPS

Heat the oil in a skillet over medium-high heat. Add the garlic and sauté for 30 seconds just to soften it. Add the collard greens, salt, and pepper, and sauté until the greens start to wilt, about 4 minutes. Add the chicken broth and simmer over low heat for 5 minutes or until tender. Drain the cooked greens and place them in a large bowl. Stir in the lemon juice, red bell pepper, apple, vinegar, and pepper flakes. The relish can be stored in an airtight container for up to 1 week.

2 tablespoons olive oil

2 garlic cloves, minced

1 bunch (about 12 stalks) collard greens, stems removed, chopped

½ teaspoon salt

¼ teaspoon freshly ground black pepper

¾ cup low-sodium chicken broth

Juice from 1 lemon

½ red bell pepper, seeded and chopped

1 Granny Smith apple, peeled, cored, and chopped

2 tablespoons white wine vinegar

¼ teaspoon red pepper flakes

Junkyard Dog

8 hot dogs

**2 cups canned chili
(from one 16-ounce can)**

**8 hot dog buns
(page 15 or store-bought)**

**8 tablespoons bacon bits
(for a real "junkyard" flair,
go with imitation bacon
bits like Bac-Os)**

**12 ounces Velveeta
cheese, melted**

**1 cup canned fried onion
rings**

You know you want it. This delicious dog is straight out of the trailer park, replete with gas-station ingredients like Velveeta and Bac-Os. It's salty, greasy transcendence for those times when that's exactly what you need—like at three a.m. . . . in Vegas . . . after you've drunk your weight in Scotch while playing black-jack. Not that we would know anything about that.

◆ ◆ ◆ ◆ ◆

Cook the hot dogs by your preferred method. Heat the chili by dumping it in a bowl and microwaving it for a couple of minutes, or dumping it into a saucepan and warming it on the stovetop. Place the hot dogs in the rolls and top each with chili, bacon bits, Velveeta, and fried onion rings. Crack open an Old Milwaukee and enjoy!

Sloppy Dog

1¼ pounds ground beef (we like 90% lean for this, since you're throwing most of the fat away, anyway)

¼ large onion, finely chopped

½ green pepper, seeded and finely chopped, divided

2 garlic cloves, minced

¾ cup ketchup (page 23 or store-bought)

1 tablespoon packed light brown sugar

1 teaspoon chili powder

½ teaspoon mustard powder

1 tablespoon tomato paste (we buy the stuff in a tube so you don't have to open a can just for one little tablespoon)

½ teaspoon Worcestershire sauce

¼ to ½ teaspoon red pepper flakes (the larger amount makes for a spicy Sloppy Joe, so use the smaller amount if you don't like heat)

¼ teaspoon salt

Freshly ground black pepper

8 potato sub rolls or hot dog buns (page 15 or store-bought)

8 hot dogs

8 ounces Muenster cheese, grated

(recipe continues)

We know you had Sloppy Joes in your school cafeteria. Maybe even your mom was the cool mom who bought Manwich and you had Sloppy Joes for dinner. Forget all of that. This is the real deal: sautéed ground beef, peppers, onions, and a magic combination of spices that puts your Sloppy Joe memories on steroids. Then you take this luscious meat concoction and pile it on top of (what else?) a hot dog, and drape the whole shebang in grated Muenster cheese. No lunch lady required.

· · ✦ ◆ ✦ · · ·

Heat a large skillet over medium-high heat and add the ground beef. Cook, breaking it up with a spoon, until the meat is universally brown. Remove the beef with a slotted spoon and set it aside in a bowl. Discard all but 1 tablespoon of the fat from the pan, and add the onions, all but 3 tablespoons of the green pepper, and the garlic. Sauté the vegetables until they are soft, about 10 minutes.

Add the ketchup, brown sugar, chili powder, mustard powder, tomato paste, Worcestershire, red pepper flakes, and ½ cup of water. Stir to combine and simmer the mixture for 15 minutes. Add the salt and pepper to taste.

Heat a second large skillet or grill pan over medium heat. Butter the insides of the rolls and toast them in the skillet. Set the rolls aside. Cook the hot dogs according to your preferred method and place them in the rolls. Top each hot dog with the Sloppy Joe mixture, some grated Muenster cheese, and some of the remaining 3 tablespoons of green pepper.

Identity Crisis Dog

Is it a wiener, or is it a hamburger? This dog can't make up its mind. It's a hot dog wrapped in ground beef and seared, but its heavenly blanket of grilled tomato-chile relish is all that really matters. The relish is more sweet and vinegary than spicy, so if you want it hotter, add the other half of the poblano pepper to the mix. And remember, your mom was right when she said it's what's on the inside that counts.

· · + + ◆ + + · ·

In a large bowl, mix together the ground beef, eggs, salt, garlic powder, and black pepper to taste. Divide the ground beef mixture into 8 even portions. Take 1 portion of beef and mold it evenly around 1 hot dog until the hot dog is completely covered by the ground beef mixture. Repeat with the other beef portions and dogs.

Heat a skillet over medium-high heat. Add the beef-wrapped dogs, being careful not to crowd the pan. (You might have to do this step in batches.) Sear the dogs all over, then lower the heat to medium-low and cover the pan to cook the meat all the way through. Add 1 or 2 tablespoons of water to the pan if it seems dry.

(recipe continues)

2 pounds ground beef (we like 85% lean for this)

3 large eggs

1 teaspoon salt

½ teaspoon garlic powder

Freshly ground black pepper

8 hot dogs

8 sub rolls

2 cups shredded sharp cheddar cheese

Grilled Tomato-Chile Relish (recipe follows)

Reserved green scallion pieces from Grilled Tomato-Chile Relish recipe

Cook the dogs for about 8 to 10 minutes. (You can insert a sharp knife into the ground beef layer to see if it's cooked all the way through.)

Meanwhile, heat another skillet over medium-high heat. Butter the insides of the sub rolls and toast them. Set the rolls aside until the dogs are done.

When the hot dogs are cooked, place them in the rolls and sprinkle them with the shredded cheese. Top with relish and garnish with the reserved green scallion pieces.

GRILLED TOMATO-CHILE RELISH

MAKES ABOUT 2 CUPS

Heat a grill or grill pan over high heat. Brush the tomatoes and pepper with oil and sprinkle with salt and pepper to taste. Grill the vegetables, turning occasionally, until they're charred in spots, about 10 minutes. Set aside to cool. In a medium bowl, whisk together the extra-virgin olive oil, vinegar, tomato paste, oregano, ¼ teaspoon of salt, ¼ teaspoon of black pepper, garlic, cinnamon, celery salt, pickle juice, and the white and light green parts of the scallions. Chop the grilled tomatoes and peppers and add them to the bowl with the dressing. Set the relish aside until ready to use. Relish can also be covered and refrigerated for up to 1 week.

3 medium plum tomatoes, sliced ½ inch thick

½ poblano pepper, seeded

Olive oil, for brushing

¼ teaspoon salt, plus more as needed

¼ teaspoon freshly ground black pepper, plus more as needed

3 tablespoons extra-virgin olive oil

1 tablespoon red wine vinegar

3 tablespoons tomato paste

½ teaspoon dried oregano

2 garlic cloves, minced

Dash of cinnamon

¼ teaspoon celery salt

1 tablespoon dill pickle juice

2 scallions, chopped, divided

Thanksgiving Dog

This is the perfect way to enjoy your leftovers when you just can't stand any more turkey. And, of course, if you want to have this at any other time of year, you can buy ready-made cranberry sauce, gravy, and stuffing to make this one easy to throw together. If the Pilgrims had had hot dogs, Turkey Day would be called Wiener Day—and that would be okay by us.

· · ✦ ◆ ✦ · ·

Split each rectangle of cornbread in half lengthwise. Melt the butter in a skillet over medium-high heat. Grill the cornbread in the butter until crisp and browned on both sides. Cook the butterflied hot dogs according to your preferred method. Top 8 of the cornbread rectangles with ¼ cup stuffing, 1 tablespoon of gravy, 1 hot dog, and ⅛ cup of cranberry sauce each. Put the other 8 rectangles on top to make sandwiches.

8 rectangles of cornbread (page 21 or store-bought), cut to approximately the same length as the hot dogs you're using

2 to 3 tablespoons unsalted butter

8 hot dogs, butterflied

2 cups prepared stuffing (leftover, store-bought, or Stove Top is fine)

8 tablespoons gravy (leftover or store-bought)

1 cup cranberry sauce (leftover or store-bought)

Boston Terrier

8 Fenway Franks or other hot dogs

8 whole wheat hot dog buns

¼ cup Irish Whiskey Mustard (page 30)

1 cup baked beans, warmed

½ large white onion, chopped

We're from the Boston area, where Fenway Franks reign supreme and Irish pubs dot every corner. This dog gilds the Beantown heritage with a little mob-style booziness, all on a whole wheat bun that would make your Irish grandmother proud.

Cook the hot dogs according to your preferred method and place them in the buns. Top with the mustard, warm baked beans, and chopped onion.

Chicken-and-Waffle Dog

3 cups all-purpose flour, divided

1 teaspoon salt, divided

½ teaspoon freshly ground black pepper

4 large eggs, divided

8 hot dogs, butterflied

2 tablespoons granulated sugar

2 teaspoons baking powder

1 teaspoon baking soda

2 cups buttermilk, well-shaken

6 tablespoons unsalted butter, melted

½ cup chopped pecans, plus more for garnish

¼ cup vegetable oil

8 tablespoons Maple Butter (recipe follows)

Chicken-fried wiener on a buttermilk-pecan waffle with maple butter? Yes, please! This salty-sweet combo is addictive, and it's as appropriate for a weekend brunch as it is for a simple Wednesday night supper. You can use frozen waffles to simplify things, but they won't be nearly as good as the homemade kind, which are super easy to make. Our recipe was inspired by one by Maggie Ruggierio in *Gourmet*. It's worth investing in a waffle iron just to make these beauties!

· · ✦ ◆ ✦ · ·

Preheat the oven to 250°F.

Place 1 cup of the flour on a plate and add ¼ teaspoon of the salt and all of the pepper. Mix well. Crack 2 eggs into a bowl and beat them together with a whisk until blended. Dredge each hot dog in the flour mixture, then in the egg, then in the flour again, and set aside.

In a large bowl, mix together the remaining 2 cups of flour, the remaining ¾ teaspoon of salt, the sugar, baking powder, and baking soda. Add the buttermilk, the remaining 2 eggs, and the butter, and mix well. Stir in the ½ cup of chopped pecans.

Heat a waffle maker according to the manufacturer's instructions and make waffles with the batter, putting each waffle on a baking sheet in the oven to keep warm while you make the rest.

Meanwhile, heat the vegetable oil in a large skillet over medium-high heat. When it is hot but not smoking, add the hot dogs, being careful not to crowd the pan. (You may need to do this in batches, depending on how large your skillet is.) Cook the hot dogs until they are browned and crisp on both sides, about 3 minutes per side.

Spread 1 tablespoon of the maple butter on each waffle, and then place 1 hot dog on top. Sprinkle with the reserved chopped pecans.

4 ounces (1 stick) unsalted butter, at room temperature

¼ cup pure maple syrup

MAPLE BUTTER

Mix the maple syrup and butter until blended.

Wake Up and Smell the Wiener

We've taken a little artistic license here and swapped out the hot dog for a breakfast sausage in order to create the most awesome wake-up wrap sandwich ever: Scrambled eggs and sausage nestled inside a fluffy homemade buttermilk pancake spread with sweet maple butter. Add a sprinkle of bacon bits and you have Sunday morning in the palm of your hand.

Brown the breakfast sausages in a skillet over medium heat. While they're browning, whisk together the eggs, milk, salt, and pepper in a medium bowl.

Melt the butter in a clean skillet (preferably nonstick) over medium heat and add the egg mixture. Stir gently to scramble the eggs.

When the eggs are about half-cooked, sprinkle the cheese over top and continue to stir until the eggs are done to your liking. Spread 1 teaspoon of maple butter on each pancake, and top with 2 sausages and a scoop of scrambled eggs.

Sprinkle the bacon crumbles on top, wrap the pancake around the filling, and repeat with the remaining ingredients. Serve immediately.

16 breakfast sausages

8 large eggs

⅓ cup milk (whole or 2%)

½ teaspoon salt

⅛ teaspoon freshly ground black pepper

1 tablespoon unsalted butter

½ cup shredded sharp cheddar cheese

8 teaspoons Maple Butter (page 60)

8 Buttermilk Pancakes (recipe follows)

4 bacon slices, cooked and crumbled

2 cups all-purpose flour

2 teaspoons baking powder

1 teaspoon baking soda

½ teaspoon salt

3 tablespoons
granulated sugar

2 large eggs, lightly beaten

3 cups buttermilk

4 tablespoons
unsalted butter, melted,
plus 1 teaspoon
for the griddle

BUTTERMILK PANCAKES

MAKES ABOUT 8 PANCAKES

In a large bowl, stir together the flour, baking powder, baking soda, salt, and sugar. Add the eggs, buttermilk, and melted butter and stir until the batter is just combined. (Do not overmix—it's fine if the batter is lumpy.)

Heat a nonstick griddle or skillet over medium-low heat until drops of water sizzle and bounce when sprinkled on it. Brush the pan with the remaining teaspoon of melted butter and drop ½ cupfuls of batter into puddles a few inches apart, working in batches. Flip the pancakes when bubbles appear on the surface and the edges start to dry. Cook for another minute or so until the other side is golden brown. Serve immediately.

SHOW DOGS

Wieners Dressed to Impress

Salty Dog

You might think clams and hot dogs are a weird combination, but trust us: This is *outrageous*. The smoky flavor of the hot dog is the perfect complement to the briny clams. It's killer with homemade fried clams, but you can use frozen ones, too. And the spicy coleslaw adds a terrific crunch and kick, with a hint of tartar sauce from the pickles. We know we're supposed to love all of our children (wieners) equally, but this hot dog is secretly the one we'd rescue from a burning building.

Place the hot dogs in the buns and top each with the coleslaw and 4 fried clams. Sprinkle a few minced pickles on top.

8 grilled hot dogs

8 hot dog buns, buttered and toasted (page 15 or store-bought)

1 batch Spicy Roasted Red Pepper Coleslaw (recipe follows)

32 fried whole-belly clams (recipe follows or frozen store-bought)

Bread and butter pickles, minced, for garnish

1/3 head red cabbage,
thinly sliced

1/3 head green cabbage,
thinly sliced

1 large carrot,
peeled and shredded

1/2 (7-ounce) jar roasted
red peppers, minced

8 bread and butter
pickle slices, minced

1 teaspoon Sriracha

1/4 teaspoon garlic powder

1 teaspoon grainy mustard

1 tablespoon
red wine vinegar

2 tablespoons mayonnaise

Salt and freshly ground
black pepper

SPICY ROASTED
RED PEPPER COLESLAW

MAKES ABOUT 3 CUPS

Mix all of the ingredients together in a large bowl. Serve immediately or cover with plastic wrap and refrigerate for up to 2 days.

CORNMEAL-CRUSTED FRIED CLAMS

MAKES 32 CLAMS

In a shallow bowl, whisk together half of the cornmeal, half of the flour, and 2 cups of water, forming a batter.

In another bowl, stir together the remaining cornmeal and flour. Dip the clams in the batter, shaking off any excess, then dredge them in the cornmeal-flour mixture to coat.

In an electric skillet or deep pot, heat the oil to 375°F. Fry the clams, a few at a time, for 4 to 5 minutes or until golden brown. Transfer the fried clams to a paper towel–lined plate, sprinkle them with salt, and serve immediately.

4½ cups yellow cornmeal, divided

1½ cups cake flour, divided

32 cherrystone or steamer clams

2 cups peanut or vegetable oil (or enough to come 2 inches up the sides of your pot)

1½ teaspoons salt

Caesar Dog

4 tablespoons unsalted
butter, at room
temperature

8 Italian sub rolls

2 teaspoons garlic powder

2 teaspoons dried oregano

2 cups freshly grated
Parmesan cheese

8 grilled hot dogs

Caesar Salad (recipe
follows)

Caesar salad is a crowd-pleaser for a reason: The garlicky, tangy crunch is wholly satisfying. And, it's even better when piled on top of a hot dog wrapped in a Parmesan crisp and lounging in garlic bread! If you don't feel like making the Caesar dressing from scratch (although, trust us, it's well worth it), just toss the lettuce with your favorite store-bought dressing.

· · ✦ ◆ ✦ ✦ · ·

Preheat the oven to 400°F.

Spread the butter on both halves of each roll, and sprinkle with garlic powder and oregano. Arrange the seasoned rolls on a baking sheet, cut side up, and bake them for 10 minutes or until they are crispy and golden brown.

Meanwhile, heat a nonstick skillet over medium heat and evenly divide half of the cheese in 4 little rounds on the hot pan. Cook the Parmesan until it melts, browns, and bubbles. (Each circle will turn into a *frico,* or cheese crisp.) Slide the crisps out of the pan and immediately wrap a hot dog in each one. Repeat with the remaining cheese. Put a crisp-wrapped hot dog in each garlic bread roll and top with Caesar salad.

1 garlic clove

2 anchovy fillets (optional)

1 large egg

3 dashes Worcestershire sauce

Juice from ½ lemon (about 1½ tablespoons)

¼ cup extra-virgin olive oil

⅛ cup freshly grated Parmesan cheese

Freshly ground black pepper

1 romaine heart, washed, dried, and thinly sliced

CAESAR SALAD

MAKES ABOUT 2 CUPS

To make the dressing, put the garlic, anchovies (if using), egg, Worcestershire, lemon juice, and 1 tablespoon of water into a blender, and process for 30 seconds or until the mixture is smooth.

With the blender running, slowly stream in the olive oil to emulsify. Stir in the Parmesan and season to taste with black pepper.

Just before assembling the dogs, put the lettuce in a bowl and add enough dressing to coat it to your liking.

Horn Dog

This wiener takes on the classic aphrodisiac combo of figs, oysters, and champagne. If you can't find champagne mustard, you can stir a splash of champagne (which you've opened already, we hope) into regular Dijon mustard. Fig jam is sold at gourmet stores or online. And it's delicious, so you should have it in your pantry to serve with cheese even when you're not making Horn Dogs.

· · + ◆ ◆ ◆ + · ·

Spread the softened butter on the sides of the hot dog buns. Place a skillet over medium heat and grill the rolls until they are lightly browned and crisp. Cook the hot dogs according to your preferred method and place them in the buns. Top each with 1 tablespoon of mustard, 5 to 6 smoked oysters, and 1 tablespoon of fig jam.

4 tablespoons unsalted butter, at room temperature

8 New England-style hot dog buns (these rolls are split on the top with soft, white sides)

8 hot dogs

8 tablespoons champagne mustard

1 (3.75-ounce) tin smoked oysters

8 tablespoons fig jam

Derby Dog

This salty Southern favorite gets a hit of sweetness from smoky bourbon–brown sugar mustard, and raw onion gives it a crunchy bite. The fact that the whole thing is piled high with sweet potato fries makes this wiener pure Thoroughbred. Trot this one out during the Kentucky Derby alongside a few mint juleps!

Bake the sweet potato fries according to the directions on the package. While they're baking, prepare the hot dogs according to your preferred method and place them in the buns. Drizzle each dog with 1 tablespoon of the mustard. Take the fries out of the oven when they're done and sprinkle them with sea salt to taste. Top each dog with ½ cup of fries and a sprinkle of chopped onion.

4 cups sweet potato fries (frozen or homemade)

8 hot dogs

8 hot dog buns (page 15 or store-bought)

8 tablespoons Bourbon–Brown Sugar Mustard (page 30)

Sea salt

½ cup chopped white onion (from about ¼ of a small onion)

Twisted Dog

A hot dog baked in homemade pretzel dough and served with a swirl of honey mustard on the side—this is a simple yet crowd-pleasing dog that will make you a hero among children. And if you bring out a tray of these bad boys during the big game? Score!

・・✦ ◆ ✦ ・・

In a medium bowl, combine the warm water with the sugar, salt, and yeast. Let the mixture sit at room temperature for about 5 minutes, or until it's foamy.

Add the flour and 4 tablespoons of the butter and mix into a rough dough. You can use a stand mixer, a food processor, or do it by hand. If you're using a stand mixer, once the dough has come together, switch to the dough hook and knead the dough on medium speed. If you're kneading by hand, turn the dough out onto a lightly floured surface and knead until it is smooth, shiny, and elastic, about 10 minutes. In a food processor, simply process the dough until it is smooth, shiny, and elastic.

(recipe continues)

1½ cups warm water

1 tablespoon granulated sugar

2 teaspoons kosher salt

2¼ teaspoons (1 packet) active dry yeast

4½ cups all-purpose flour

6 tablespoons unsalted butter, melted and divided

⅔ cup baking soda

8 hot dogs

Coarse sea salt, for sprinkling

Honey Mustard (page 30)

Transfer the dough to a greased bowl, cover it with plastic wrap, and place it in a warm area to rise for about 1 hour, or until the dough has doubled in size. If you want to make the dough ahead of time, you can put it in the refrigerator for a slow rise and use it after 12 hours or up to 3 days later.

Preheat the oven to 400°F. Line a baking sheet with parchment paper.

Mix the baking soda and 10 cups of water in a large pot and bring the mixture to a boil over medium-high heat. Divide the prepared dough into 8 equal pieces. Roll each piece of dough into a rope about 24 inches long. Wrap a rope of dough around each hot dog in a spiral. Gently drop the hot dogs into the boiling water two at a time and boil them for 30 seconds. Remove them from the water and place them on the prepared baking sheet.

When all the hot dogs have been boiled, brush the tops with the remaining 2 tablespoons of melted butter and sprinkle them with the salt.

Bake the dogs until the pretzel dough is dark brown, about 10 to 15 minutes. Slide the parchment off the baking sheet onto a counter or wire rack to cool slightly before serving. Serve with honey mustard.

Mardi Gras Dog

This dog pays homage to classic New Orleans cuisine. It consists of a spicy andouille sausage topped with blackened shrimp, drizzled with creamy, savory rémoulade, and sprinkled with chopped celery for crunch. (As a bonus, the leftover sauce is great on sandwiches, as a dip for crudités, or even drizzled on chicken or fish.) If you can't get to the Big Easy for Fat Tuesday, throw your own parade with these wieners.

60 medium (1 pound) uncooked shrimp, peeled and deveined

1 tablespoon paprika

1 teaspoon garlic powder

1 teaspoon onion powder

¼ teaspoon cayenne pepper

2 teaspoons freshly ground black pepper

½ teaspoon dried thyme leaves

½ teaspoon dried oregano

1 tablespoon vegetable oil

8 sub rolls, with the ends trimmed to fit the sausages

8 andouille sausages, butterflied

8 tablespoons rémoulade (recipe follows)

2 celery stalks, chopped

1 lemon, cut into 8 wedges

(recipe continues)

Put the shrimp in a bowl and toss them with the paprika, garlic powder, onion powder, cayenne pepper, black pepper, thyme, and oregano.

Heat the oil in a skillet over medium-high heat. Add the shrimp and sauté until they are opaque and cooked through. Cook the andouille sausages by your preferred method.

Put 3 to 4 shrimp in each sub roll, and top with 1 sausage, 1 tablespoon of rémoulade, and 4 to 5 more shrimp. Sprinkle with the chopped celery. Serve each dog with a wedge of lemon for spritzing.

1 cup mayonnaise

2 tablespoons Dijon mustard

Juice from ½ small lemon (about 1 tablespoon)

1 small handful flat-leaf parsley leaves

1 tablespoon Louisiana-style hot sauce (like Frank's RedHot)

2 teaspoons whole grain mustard

2 garlic cloves

2 teaspoons capers

1 teaspoon Worcestershire sauce

1 teaspoon paprika

1 scallion, white and light green parts, chopped

¼ teaspoon kosher salt

⅛ teaspoon cayenne pepper

RÉMOULADE

MAKES ABOUT 1¼ CUPS

Place all of the ingredients in a food processor or blender and pulse to combine. The rémoulade tastes best if refrigerated for 1 hour before serving, and it will keep in the refrigerator for up to 1 week in an airtight container.

Apple Pie Dog

Combining hot dogs with apple pie—how American can you get? Here, a hot dog is topped with a savory mixture of sautéed apples, onions, and thyme, drizzled with ginger honey mustard, and baked in a piecrust—the perfect dog to make on a crisp fall day after apple picking. Be sure the apple-onion mixture is cooled to room temperature before assembling, as the pastry needs to stay cold for it to emerge from the oven flaky and delicious.

· · ✦ ✦ ✦ ✦ · ·

Melt the butter in a large skillet over medium heat and add the apples and onions. Sauté the apples and onions until they are soft and begin to brown, about 10 minutes. Stir in the thyme and season to taste with salt and pepper. Remove the pan from the heat and set it aside to cool.

Stir the ginger into the honey mustard and set it aside.

Preheat the oven to 400°F. Line a large baking sheet with parchment paper.

(recipe continues)

2 tablespoons unsalted butter

2 Granny Smith apples, peeled, cored, and chopped

2 medium onions, chopped

¼ teaspoon dried thyme

Salt and freshly ground black pepper

1 teaspoon peeled and freshly grated ginger, or ¼ teaspoon ground ginger

6 tablespoons Honey Mustard (page 30)

Savory Piecrust (recipe follows or 1 package store-bought piecrust)

8 hot dogs

When the apple-onion mixture is cool, roll out the piecrust until it is ¼ inch thick. Cut the dough into 8 rectangles.

Place 1 hot dog, 1 spoonful of apple-onion mixture, and a drizzle of mustard onto each piecrust rectangle. Roll the crust around the hot dog to make a tight bundle, and place the bundles on the prepared baking sheet.

Bake the hot dogs until the crust is browned, about 30 minutes.

"I love hot dogs anywhere."

—Jacques Pépin

SAVORY PIECRUST

MAKES ABOUT 1 PIECRUST
or enough for 8 Apple Pie Dogs

2½ cups all-purpose flour, divided

1 teaspoon salt

6 ounces (1½ sticks) cold unsalted butter, cut into tablespoon-size chunks

½ cup cold vegetable shortening, cut into 4 pieces

¼ cup cold vodka

¼ cup ice water

This piecrust recipe is a miracle developed by the food scientists at *Cook's Illustrated*. The vodka is not a misprint. It adds liquid to the dough, which makes it easy to work with, but evaporates in the oven, unlike water, yielding a more tender crust. If you don't have any, you can substitute water, but your crust won't be as good.

In the bowl of a food processor, pulse together 1½ cups of the flour and the salt. Add the butter and shortening and process until the dough starts to clump up. (You can also do this by hand in a bowl with a pastry blender or two knives. Simply mix the dough until all the flour is coated with fat and it's forming clumps.)

Add the remaining 1 cup of flour and pulse until the dough breaks up, about 5 quick pulses. (Or mix in the flour by hand, breaking up the dough with your two knives or pastry blender.)

Add the vodka and ice water and pulse until you have a ball of moist dough, about 5 more pulses. (Or, stir in the liquids by hand with a rubber spatula.)

Form the dough into two disks, wrap them in plastic wrap, and refrigerate them for at least 1 hour before using. You can also make this ahead of time and keep it in the fridge for a few days or in the freezer for 1 month.

BLT Dog

8 slices of bacon

8 hot dogs

8 hot dog buns
(page 15 or store-bought)

8 tablespoons
Garlic-Peppercorn Aioli
(recipe follows)

1 heart of romaine lettuce,
chopped

2 medium tomatoes,
chopped

This dog comes together really quickly and will delight anyone who loves BLTs, which, of course, is everyone. The Garlic-Peppercorn Aioli is super-easy to make and light-years above regular mayo. Use any leftover aioli to make a killer tuna or chicken salad.

• • • ✦ ✦ ✦ • • •

Spiral-wrap 1 bacon slice around each hot dog.

Fry the bacon-wrapped hot dogs in a large skillet over medium heat until the bacon is cooked all over, about 10 minutes.

Spread 1 tablespoon of the aioli on each hot dog roll, top with romaine lettuce, and place a bacon-wrapped hot dog inside. Top with the chopped tomatoes.

½ teaspoon black peppercorns, crushed

½ cup mayonnaise

1 garlic clove, minced

¾ teaspoon grated lemon zest

1 teaspoon freshly squeezed lemon juice

GARLIC-PEPPERCORN AIOLI

MAKES ABOUT ½ CUP

Mix all the ingredients together in a bowl, cover with plastic wrap, and refrigerate for up to 1 week.

Wiener Wellington

Beef Wellington is the dinner of royalty: a perfectly rare beef tenderloin tucked inside rich, crisp puff pastry and bathed in a delectable mushroom duxelles. Although the real deal is kind of tricky to pull off, it's really easy to make a hot dog version at home, because the glorious tube steak is already cooked, eliminating most of the trickiness. The only critical rule is that all the ingredients must be cold when you're assembling the Wellingtons; otherwise, the pastry won't puff in the oven.

· · ◆ ◆ ◆ ◆ ◆ · ·

Preheat the oven to 400°F. Line a baking sheet with parchment.

On a floured surface, roll out the puff pastry and cut it into 6 rectangles, each roughly an inch longer than the hot dogs. Place a hot dog in the center of each rectangle and cover it with mushroom duxelles. Wrap the puff pastry around the hot dog, completely enclosing it.

Place the puff pastry bundles onto the prepared baking sheet.

Whisk the egg with a splash of water to make an egg wash. Brush the puff pastry bundles with the egg wash and transfer the baking sheet to the oven.

Bake for 25 to 30 minutes or until the pastry is puffed and browned.

1 sheet frozen puff pastry, thawed

6 cold hot dogs

2 cups Red Wine Mushroom Duxelles (recipe follows), chilled

1 large egg

RED WINE MUSHROOM DUXELLES

2 tablespoons unsalted butter

1 pound button mushrooms, finely diced (about 4 cups)

1 shallot, minced

1 cup dry red wine

1 teaspoon chopped fresh thyme, or ½ teaspoon dried thyme

Salt and freshly ground black pepper

Melt the butter in a skillet over medium heat. Add the mushrooms and shallot and sauté until the vegetables are soft, about 5 minutes. Add the wine and bring the mixture to a simmer. Reduce the heat and simmer until all the liquid is absorbed, about 20 minutes. Remove the pan from the heat, stir in the thyme, and season to taste with salt and pepper.

DOGS
THAT BITE

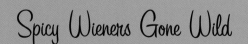

Spicy Wieners Gone Wild

HOT Dog

This one is for all the spicy food lovers! First, we fry up some jalapeño slices. Then, we rub the hot dogs with a spice mixture, brown them, place them in garlic-Tabasco buttered buns, and top the whole thing with spicy Sriracha mustard! It's got levels of heat and flavor that will thrill anyone who loves the sweet burn of chilies. If you want to skip the deep-frying step, you can use fresh jalapeño slices instead.

· · · ◆ ◆ ◆ · · ·

Heat the oil in a large deep pot to 375°F. (You need a frying thermometer for this. You can buy one at any grocery store.)

Dip the jalapeño slices into the flour. Fry the jalapeños until they are lightly browned and crisp, 1 to 2 minutes, then transfer them to a paper towel–lined plate to drain while you prepare the dogs.

Combine the cayenne, paprika, 1 teaspoon of garlic powder, and chili powder in a small bowl. Rub the hot dogs with the spice mixture.

Melt 1 tablespoon of the butter in a skillet over medium-high heat. Cook the hot dogs in the skillet until they are browned and

(recipe continues)

2 cups peanut or vegetable oil

4 jalapeño peppers, sliced

¼ cup all-purpose flour

½ teaspoon cayenne pepper

1 teaspoon paprika

1½ teaspoons garlic powder, divided

1 teaspoon chili powder

8 hot dogs

5 tablespoons unsalted butter, divided

1 teaspoon Tabasco sauce

8 New England–style hot dog buns

½ cup coarse ground mustard

1 tablespoon Sriracha or other hot sauce

fragrant, about 5 minutes. Wipe out the skillet and return it to the stove. Melt the remaining butter with the remaining garlic powder and Tabasco in a small saucepan. (Alternatively, you can melt the mixture together in a bowl in the microwave.) Brush the melted butter mixture on the sides of the hot dog buns and toast them in the skillet over medium heat.

Mix the mustard and Sriracha together in a small bowl. Place the hot dogs in the buns and drizzle them with the mustard. Top with the fried jalapeño slices.

Soul Dog

First of all, we're talking about homemade buttermilk biscuit buns here. Just about anything you put on that will rock your world. But when it's a hot dog and spicy bacon-barbecued onions, all nestled on a fluffy bed of cheesy grits? *Yee-haw!*

Melt the butter in a medium frying pan and add the onions. Sauté over medium heat until the onions are translucent and soft and beginning to brown, about 5 minutes. Mix in the barbecue sauce and crumbled bacon, and keep the mixture warm over low heat while you cook the hot dogs. Cook the hot dogs according to your preferred method. Split open each biscuit bun and top each with a hot dog, ½ cup of grits, and a spoonful of barbecued onions. Place the other half of the biscuit bun on top.

1 tablespoon unsalted butter

1 large onion, thinly sliced

½ cup barbecue sauce (page 26 or store-bought)

4 bacon slices, cooked and crumbled

8 hot dogs, butterflied

8 freshly made Buttermilk Biscuit Buns (page 17)

4 cups Cheesy Grits (recipe follows)

CHEESY GRITS

MAKES ABOUT 4 CUPS

Combine the milk, 2 cups of water, and the salt in a large pot over medium-high heat and bring the mixture to a boil. Gradually whisk in the cornmeal. Once all the cornmeal has been incorporated, turn the heat to low and cover the pot. Cook for 20 to 25 minutes, whisking every few minutes to prevent lumps, until the mixture is creamy.

Remove the pot from the heat, add the pepper and butter, and whisk to combine. Once the butter is melted, gradually whisk in the cheese a little at a time. Serve immediately.

2 cups whole milk

1½ teaspoons kosher salt

1 cup coarsely ground cornmeal

½ teaspoon freshly ground black pepper

4 tablespoons unsalted butter, at room temperature

1 cup shredded sharp cheddar cheese

Cowboy Up! Dog

8 hot dogs

8 hot dog buns
(page 15 or store-bought)

2 cups Texas Chili
(recipe follows)

2 cups shredded sharp
cheddar cheese

3 scallions, light and dark
green parts sliced

This is a classic chili dog, with spicy (and easy-to-make) Texas chili, sharp Cheddar cheese, and scallions. The chili does not have beans, in authentic Texas fashion, but feel free to throw in some kidney beans if you live outside the Lone Star State.

· · ◆ ◆ ◆ ◆ · ·

Cook the hot dogs according to your preferred method, and place them in the buns. Top each with ¼ cup of the chili, ¼ cup of the shredded cheddar, and a sprinkle of chopped scallions.

1 pound ground beef
(we like 90% lean for this)

1 large onion, chopped

6 garlic cloves, minced

2 jalapeño peppers,
seeded and chopped

1 (16-ounce) can
tomato sauce

1 (28-ounce) can
crushed tomatoes

2 teaspoons ground cumin

3 tablespoons chili
powder

1 teaspoon salt

TEXAS CHILI

MAKES 4 SERVINGS
or enough for 8 Cowboy Up! Dogs with leftovers

Brown the ground beef in a large pot over medium-high heat. Add the onions, garlic, and peppers, and sauté until the vegetables start to soften, about 10 minutes. Add all of the remaining ingredients, and bring the chili to a simmer. Reduce the heat to low and simmer the chili for 30 minutes to blend the flavors and thicken it. Serve immediately.

Wiener au Poivre

Steak au poivre is a classic French bistro staple, and for good reason. The crunch and bite of the peppercorns, the savory meat, and the rich, creamy sauce combine to form a uniquely satisfying dish. When this same technique is applied to the almighty wiener, magic occurs.

· + ♦ ♦ ♦ + ·

Preheat the oven to 400°F. Put the peppercorns in a zip-top bag and crush them with a mallet or other heavy object, then dump them onto a shallow plate. Press each butterflied hot dog into the crushed peppercorns, pushing down so the peppercorns adhere.

Melt 1 tablespoon of the butter and add the oil in a large skillet over medium-high heat. Sear the hot dogs until they are browned on both sides; remove them from the skillet, and set them aside. Melt the rest of the butter in the skillet and add the shallots. Sauté the shallots until they are softened, about 3 minutes.

(recipe continues)

½ cup whole black peppercorns, crushed

8 hot dogs, butterflied

4 tablespoons unsalted butter, divided

1 tablespoon vegetable oil

2 shallots, minced

½ cup cognac

¾ cup heavy whipping cream

2 baguettes

Add the cognac and boil for 1 minute, scraping up any brown bits from the bottom of the skillet. Add the cream and cook until the sauce is thickened, about 2 minutes.

Split each baguette three-quarters of the way through lengthwise and cut each into 4 pieces. Place the baguette pieces directly on the oven rack and toast until they are light golden brown and crisp. Remove baguette pieces from the oven, top them with the hot dogs, and drizzle the sauce on top.

> *"The noblest of all dogs is the hot dog; it feeds the hand that bites it."*
>
> —Lawrence J. Peter

Buffalo Dog

4 ounces (1 stick) unsalted butter

1 cup hot sauce (like Frank's RedHot), plus more for drizzling

1 teaspoon cayenne pepper

8 hot dogs, butterflied

8 slices white sandwich bread

1 cup chunky blue cheese dressing

4 celery stalks, chopped

If you like Buffalo wings, you'll love this dog. Grilled and mopped with a three-ingredient homemade Buffalo sauce, then smothered in blue cheese dressing with celery for crunch, this dog is better than anything you'll find in a sports bar. Even if you're from Buffalo. We like it on plain white sandwich bread, but you can throw it into a bun if you desire.

⋯ ✦ ✦ ◆ ✦ ✦ ⋯

Melt the butter in a small skillet over medium heat and mix in the hot sauce and cayenne pepper. Butterfly and grill the hot dogs. Place each hot dog on a slice of white bread and drizzle with the hot sauce. Top with some blue cheese dressing and chopped celery. Wrap the bread around the filling like a taco and enjoy.

Hair of the Dog

Ah, the morning after. When you wake up with a pounding head and shaky hands, what you need is a little of the hair of the dog that bit you, this time in the form of bourbon ketchup drizzled on top of spicy sausage and hash browns. This recipe is easy enough to make with half-closed eyes and one hand clutching a coffee mug. It will cure what ails you—and the seven friends who crashed at your place last night.

Brown the sausages in a skillet over medium heat until cooked through, about 15 minutes. Meanwhile, melt the butter in another skillet, add the oil, and sauté the hash browns with the red pepper flakes until they are crisp and browned, about 10 minutes. Combine the ketchup and the bourbon in a small saucepan and bring the mixture to a boil. Let it simmer for 5 minutes.

Place the sausages in the sub rolls, top with the hash browns, and drizzle with the bourbon ketchup.

8 hot Italian sausages

2 tablespoons unsalted butter

2 tablespoons vegetable oil

1 (20-ounce) bag shredded hash browns, thawed if frozen

¼ teaspoon red pepper flakes

½ cup Ketchup (page 23 or store-bought)

2 tablespoons bourbon

8 sub rolls

Dogbreath Dog

2 heads garlic

4 tablespoons plus 1 teaspoon olive oil, divided

Fine sea salt

4 tablespoons unsalted butter

2 baguettes

1 cup Honey Mustard (page 30)

4 garlic cloves, minced or crushed through a press

8 hot dogs

2 scallions, thinly sliced (green parts only)

This one is for garlic lovers! If you're a fan of the "stinking rose," look no further than the Dogbreath Dog. It calls for a lot of garlic, but don't worry, most of it is roasted, which mellows and sweetens the flavor. Still, we don't recommend this one for a first date.

· · · ✦ ◆ ✦ · · ·

Preheat the oven to 400°F.

Slice off and discard the top quarter of each head of garlic and place the heads on a square of aluminum foil, cut-sides up. Drizzle the garlic with 1 teaspoon of the olive oil and sprinkle with salt to taste. Seal the foil around the garlic and roast the garlic in the oven for 30 minutes or until it is very soft.

In a small saucepan over medium heat, melt the butter with the remaining 4 tablespoons of olive oil and add 2 cloves of the roasted garlic. Mash the garlic into the butter-oil mixture until the mixture is smooth, and season with salt to taste. Split the baguettes three-quarters of the way through lengthwise and smear the insides with the garlic butter. Put the garlic bread in the oven and toast until lightly browned and crisp, about 10 minutes.

(recipe continues)

In a small bowl, mix the honey mustard with the fresh minced or crushed garlic.

Cook the hot dogs by your preferred method. Cut the baguettes into 4 pieces each. Place a hot dog in each roll, top with a few cloves of roasted garlic, and drizzle with the honey-garlic mustard. Sprinkle with the sliced scallions.

> *"Some people wanted champagne and caviar when they should have had beer and hot dogs."*
>
> **—Dwight D. Eisenhower**

Nacho Mama's Dog

This dog is like a pile of the best nachos you've ever had. We recommend butterflying the hot dogs so they can hold more stuff. Because, after all, isn't that the whole point of nachos?

· · ◆ ◆ ◆ ◆ · ·

Cook the hot dogs according to your preferred method.

Spread 2 tablespoons of guacamole on each hot dog roll and place the hot dogs on top. On top of each hot dog add 2 tablespoons of salsa, 1 tablespoon of chopped olives, 2 tablespoons of melted Velveeta, and 1 tablespoon of onions. Finally, pile ½ cup of crushed tortilla chips on top of each hot dog. Serve with sour cream and hot sauce on the side.

8 hot dogs, butterflied

1 cup Guacamole (recipe follows or store-bought)

8 hot dog buns (page 15 or store-bought)

1 cup Fresh Salsa (recipe follows or store-bought)

8 tablespoons chopped black olives

1 cup Velveeta cheese, melted

8 tablespoons chopped yellow onion (from about ½ small onion)

2 cups crushed tortilla chips

Sour cream, for serving

Hot sauce, for serving

GUACAMOLE

MAKES ABOUT 2 CUPS

Mash tomato, onion, chiles, lime juice, and salt in a bowl with a fork. Scoop the flesh from the avocados and add to the bowl along with the cilantro. Mix and mash together, leaving some lumps. Serve immediately.

1 medium tomato, finely chopped

2 tablespoons minced white onion

2 serrano chiles, finely chopped

1 tablespoon fresh lime juice

2 large avocados, pitted

2 tablespoons chopped cilantro

3 medium tomatoes,
chopped

½ cup finely chopped
white onion

2 jalapeno peppers
(with seeds), finely chopped

½ cup chopped
fresh cilantro

1 teaspoon salt

2 teaspoons fresh lime juice

FRESH SALSA

MAKES ABOUT 3 CUPS

Mix all ingredients in a bowl. Chill in refrigerator for 1 hour to blend flavors, and for up to 3 days.

DOGS *with* PASSPORTS

Wild Wieners
From Around the World

Weenie Rangoon

You've had crab rangoon at Chinese restaurants. Well, forget about that, because after you've had Weenie Rangoon, things will never be the same again. Our recipe isn't totally authentic (and how authentic is crab rangoon, anyway?), but the roasted garlic gives it a sweet richness, and the dipping sauce is an extra step that is more than worth it. Serve these at your next party and watch them disappear.

· · ✦ ✦ ◆ ✦ ✦ · ·

Preheat the oven to 400°F.

Slice off the top quarter of the garlic head and place it on a square of aluminum foil. Drizzle the garlic with the oil. Wrap the foil around the garlic and bake the garlic for approximately 30 minutes, or until it's very soft.

Squeeze the cloves out of the skins into a bowl. Mash the garlic with a fork. Add the ginger, scallions, sesame oil, and vinegar. Mix together.

Evenly divide the spice paste among the egg roll wrappers, spooning it into the center of each one. Place 1 hot dog piece on

(recipe continues)

1 head garlic

1 tablespoon olive oil

1 teaspoon peeled and freshly grated ginger (or ¼ teaspoon dried ginger)

3 scallions, white and light green parts, chopped

1 tablespoon sesame oil

1 teaspoon rice vinegar

24 egg roll wrappers

8 hot dogs, cut into thirds

4 cups peanut or vegetable oil (or enough to come 2 inches up the sides of your pot)

Rangoon Sauce, for serving (recipe follows)

top of each mound of spice paste and fold the egg roll wrapper around it, twisting it at the top to make a little bundle. Repeat with the remaining hot dogs and egg roll wrappers.

Heat the peanut or vegetable oil in a large, deep pot to 375°F.

Fry the bundles a few at a time, being careful not to crowd the pot, until they're browned and crisp, about 1 minute. Transfer the cooked bundles to a paper towel–lined plate. When all the rangoons are fried, serve them immediately with the sauce for dipping.

RANGOON SAUCE

Mix all the ingredients together in a bowl.

½ cup plum sauce (found in the Asian section of the grocery store)

1 tablespoon low-sodium soy sauce

½ cup rice vinegar

1 tablespoon Dijon mustard

1 scallion, white and light green parts, chopped

1 teaspoon peeled and grated fresh ginger (or ¼ teaspoon dried ginger)

½ teaspoon red pepper flakes

Bark Bourguignon

1 tablespoon unsalted butter

2 cups pearl onions, peeled (thawed, if frozen)

2 cups sliced button mushrooms

8 hot dogs, butterflied

8 popovers (page 20)

4 cups Red Wine-Braised Short Ribs (recipe follows)

¼ cup chopped flat-leaf parsley, for garnish

Boeuf bourguignon is a classic French stew of braised beef, mushrooms, and onions cooked in red wine. Often, it starts with bacon, but the smokiness in this version is provided by the wiener. This version is made with short ribs, which result in silky, tender meat after braising. We drape them on top of a hot dog with sautéed mushrooms and pearl onions, and nestle the whole thing into a popover, creating a meal that's both impressive and comforting, like all the best French food.

﹢ ﹢ ﹢ ◆ ◆ ﹢ ﹢ ﹢

Melt the butter over medium heat in a frying pan. Add the onions and sauté until they are soft, about 10 minutes. Add the mushrooms and cook until they are soft and both vegetables are beginning to brown, about another 5 to 10 minutes.

Cook the hot dogs according to your preferred method. Split the popovers open and place the hot dogs inside. Place ½ cup of the mushroom-onion mixture and ½ cup of the braised meat on top of each hot dog. Sprinkle each hot dog with chopped parsley.

4 pounds beef short ribs

2 teaspoons kosher salt

1 teaspoon freshly
ground black pepper

1 tablespoon vegetable oil

4 garlic cloves, chopped

1 medium yellow onion,
chopped

4 carrots, peeled
and chopped

3 celery stalks, chopped

2 cups dry red wine

1½ cups low-sodium
beef broth

1 tablespoon chopped
fresh rosemary

1 teaspoon chopped
fresh thyme

½ cup tomato paste

1 teaspoon pure maple syrup

RED WINE–BRAISED
SHORT RIBS

MAKES 4 CUPS

Preheat the oven to 300°F.

Sprinkle the short ribs with the salt and pepper. Heat the oil in a large ovenproof pot or Dutch oven over high heat. Sear the ribs all over until dark brown, about 10 minutes, and then transfer them to a platter. Reduce the heat to medium and add the garlic, onion, carrots, and celery. Sauté the vegetables until they are soft and starting to brown, about 5 minutes.

Add the wine and beef broth, scraping up the brown bits from the bottom of the pot, and then add the rosemary, thyme, tomato paste, and maple syrup; stir to combine. Return the short ribs to the pot and cover tightly.

Place the pot in the oven and braise the ribs for approximately 2 hours or until the meat is tender and falling off the bone. Serve immediately, or cool to room temperature, then cover and refrigerate for up to 3 days.

Fifi

This is a decadent and oh-so-French wiener that is right at home next to a glass of Champagne. The fried leeks add spectacular crunch and flavor to this dog and are worth the extra step. The tiny French poodle in your purse is optional.

· · ◆ ◆ ◆ · ·

Heat 1 inch of oil in a large pot over medium-high heat. When the oil is hot but not smoking, carefully add the leeks and fry them until they are golden brown and crisp, about 1 minute. Set aside.

Preheat the oven to 400°F. Cook the hot dogs according to your preferred method. Cut each baguette into 4 pieces cross-wise and split each piece three-quarters of the way through lengthwise. Place the baguette pieces directly on the oven rack and toast them until they are golden brown and crisp, about 5 minutes. Spread each baguette piece with 1½ tablespoons of the mustard. Top each with a hot dog.

Slice the Brie and pâté into 8 equal portions each and place 1 slice of each on each hot dog. Sprinkle the fried leeks on top.

Canola or peanut oil

1 leek, white and light green part only, thinly sliced

8 hot dogs, butterflied

2 baguettes

¾ cup coarse brown mustard

12 ounces Brie cheese

8 ounces goose or duck liver pâté

Tiki Terrier

1/4 cup orange juice

1 tablespoon low-sodium
soy sauce

1 tablespoon packed
dark brown sugar

1 garlic clove, minced
or crushed through a press

1 teaspoon sesame oil

1 teaspoon peeled
and freshly grated ginger

8 hot dogs

8 hot dog buns
(page 15 or store-bought)

2 cups Grilled Pineapple
Salsa (recipe follows)

When we gave a WGW party to benefit our local elementary school, the Tiki Terrier was the favorite dog, hands down. The hot dogs are marinated in a simple homemade teriyaki sauce, then topped with a sweet-spicy grilled pineapple salsa. Umbrella drinks are optional, but highly recommended.

· · + · ◆ · + · ·

In a large zip-top bag, combine the orange juice, soy sauce, brown sugar, garlic, sesame oil, and ginger. Add the hot dogs, tightly seal the bag closed, and shake to coat the hot dogs in the marinade. (If you have time, let them marinate in the fridge for up to 8 hours.) Grill the hot dogs, place them in the buns, and top them with the salsa.

1 (20-ounce) can sliced
pineapple

2 jalapeño peppers,
seeded and minced

2 garlic cloves, minced
or crushed through a press

½ large red onion,
chopped

1 teaspoon peeled
and freshly grated ginger

⅛ cup chopped fresh
cilantro

Juice from ½ lime

Salt and freshly ground
black pepper

GRILLED PINEAPPLE SALSA

MAKES ABOUT 3 CUPS

Grill the pineapple slices on a grill or grill pan over high heat until they're caramelized, about 1 minute on each side. Chop the pineapple and transfer it to a medium bowl. Mix in all of the other ingredients and season to taste with salt and pepper.

German Shepherd's Pie

A deconstructed shepherd's pie adorning a bratwurst—it's Oktoberfest, even if it's July! You can peel the potatoes, if you like; we like the skins, so we kept them on for this recipe. Don't let the long ingredients list intimidate you. This recipe has three distinct components (mashed potatoes, beef with apple cider gravy, and sweet corn relish), but it comes together quickly. You can make the relish while the potatoes boil, and make the gravy while you grill the brats. It's easy as shepherd's pie.

Cook the brats according to your preferred method, and put them in the rolls. Top with gravy, potatoes, and relish.

8 bratwursts

8 crusty sub rolls

**Beef with Apple Cider Gravy
(recipe follows)**

**Mashed Potatoes
(recipe follows)**

**Sweet Corn Relish
(recipe follows)**

MASHED POTATOES

4 medium red-skinned potatoes, quartered

1/3 cup half-and-half

4 tablespoons unsalted butter

1 teaspoon fine sea salt

Freshly ground black pepper

Put the potatoes in a medium stockpot or saucepan and cover them with cold water. Bring the water to a boil and boil the potatoes until they are tender, about 20 minutes.

Meanwhile, combine the half-and-half, butter, salt, and pepper to taste in a small saucepan over low heat. Drain the potatoes and return them to the hot pot to dry them out for a bit. Add the butter mixture and mash the potatoes with a potato masher until they are smooth and fluffy. Keep the mashed potatoes warm while you prepare the other components.

1 tablespoon olive oil

1 teaspoon unsalted butter

½ medium yellow onion,
finely chopped

½ red bell pepper,
seeded and finely chopped

1 (1-pound) bag frozen
sweet corn

2 garlic cloves, minced

¼ teaspoon salt

Freshly ground black pepper

Dash of freshly grated
or ground nutmeg

1 teaspoon pure maple syrup

SWEET CORN RELISH

MAKES ABOUT 3 CUPS

Heat a medium skillet over medium-high heat. Add the oil and butter, and when the butter is melted, add the onion and red pepper. Sauté the vegetables until they are soft, about 10 minutes. Add the corn and garlic and sauté the entire mixture for another 5 minutes, or until the corn is thawed and heated through. Add the salt, pepper to taste, nutmeg, and maple syrup. Adjust the seasonings as necessary.

BEEF WITH APPLE CIDER GRAVY

MAKES ABOUT 3 CUPS

1 tablespoon cornstarch

½ cup apple cider

1 teaspoon olive oil

½ medium yellow onion, finely chopped

1 pound ground beef (we like 90% lean for this)

In a medium bowl, dissolve the cornstarch in the apple cider and set the mixture aside at room temperature. Heat the oil in a medium skillet over medium-high heat. Add the onion and sauté until it is translucent, about 10 minutes. Add the ground beef and sauté it, breaking it up with a spoon, until it is no longer pink. Using a slotted spoon, transfer the beef to a bowl, and pour off all but 1 tablespoon of fat from the pan.

Add the cornstarch-cider mixture and cook, scraping up any brown bits from the bottom of the pan, until the gravy is thickened. Return the beef to the pan and mix well to combine.

Quesadilla Dog

We threw out the bun on this one and swapped it for a spicy, cheesy quesadilla, thereby creating the ultimate comfort food. The smoky, salty hot dog is the perfect complement to the sautéed onions and peppers and the sharp cheese. These are very easy to put together and make a great lunch, dinner, or midnight snack. Once you try this, you'll never want an ordinary quesadilla again.

Heat the oil in a large skillet over medium heat and add the peppers and onions. Sauté until the onions and peppers are soft and starting to brown, about 10 minutes. Add the garlic and cook for 2 more minutes. Divide the onion-pepper mixture among 8 tortillas. Sprinkle 2 tablespoons of Monterey Jack cheese and 2 tablespoons of cheddar cheese evenly over each of the 8 tortillas. Top each with another tortilla to make a sandwich.

Preheat the oven to 200°F.

Heat the butter in a skillet over medium heat. Cook each quesadilla in the skillet, turning once, until the cheese is melted. Place the cooked quesadillas on a baking sheet and place them in the oven to keep warm while you cook the remaining quesadillas. Cook the hot dogs according to your preferred method, and wrap a quesadilla around each hot dog. Serve with sour cream and pico de gallo.

1 tablespoon vegetable oil

2 cups sliced green chile peppers (like poblano), with seeds

2 medium onions, sliced

1 garlic clove, chopped

16 corn tortillas

1 cup shredded Monterey Jack cheese

1 cup shredded sharp cheddar cheese

2 tablespoons unsalted butter

8 hot dogs

Sour cream, for serving

Prepared pico de gallo or fresh salsa, for serving

Chi-Wow-Wow

An homage to classic Mexican street food, this dog is topped with grilled corn that's been slathered with cilantro, butter, and lime, and then topped with queso fresco. Queso fresco is a salty, soft Mexican cheese that is very similar to feta. This dog is easy to put together and great for a Cinco de Mayo party—just add margaritas!

Heat a grill or grill pan over high heat. Brush the corn with the oil and grill it until it loses its raw appearance and black and brown grill marks appear, about 5 to 7 minutes. Remove the corn from the heat and cut the kernels from the cobs into a bowl. Add the butter, cilantro, and lime juice to the corn, and mix well. Cook the hot dogs according to your preferred method, and place them in the buns. Divide the corn among the hot dogs and sprinkle each with 1 teaspoon of queso fresco and some chopped tomatoes.

4 ears corn on the cob, husked

1 tablespoon vegetable oil

2 tablespoons unsalted butter, melted

¼ cup chopped fresh cilantro

Juice of 1 lime (about 2 tablespoons)

8 hot dogs

8 hot dog buns (page 15 or store-bought)

8 teaspoons queso fresco (found in the cheese section of the grocery store, or at Latino markets)

2 plum tomatoes, chopped

Paella Dog

8 chorizo sausages, butterflied

8 sub rolls

1 (14-ounce) box Spanish yellow rice mix, prepared

8 tablespoons Sofrito (recipe follows)

We love paella—we love to eat it, we love to make it, we love to watch other people eat it and make it—and you'll love us after you try it. A chorizo sausage topped with Spanish rice and sofrito sauce will remind you of the best paella you ever had, and maybe make you wish you lived in Spain, where they eat like this all the time.

· · ◆ ◆ ◆ ◆ · ·

Cook the chorizo according to your preferred method. (We fry ours in a pan with a little oil.) Place the sausages in the rolls, top each with a few spoonfuls of rice, and then drizzle each with 1 tablespoon of sofrito.

1 tablespoon
extra-virgin olive oil

1 long sweet green pepper,
seeded and chopped

1 medium yellow
onion, chopped

2 large garlic cloves, minced

1 (28-ounce) can
crushed tomatoes

1 teaspoon paprika

Salt and freshly ground
black pepper

SOFRITO

MAKES ABOUT 4 CUPS

Heat the olive oil in a large frying pan over medium heat and add the peppers and onions. Sauté the vegetables until they are transparent and soft, about 10 minutes. Add the garlic and sauté for 1 minute. Add the remaining ingredients and bring the mixture to a simmer. Continue simmering the mixture for about 15 minutes.

Rasta Dog

Jamaica, mon! This dog celebrates the flavors of Jamaica with a spicy-sweet jerk rub, fried bananas, and curry mustard. So put on some reggae, crack open a Red Stripe, and make it happen.

1 tablespoon ground allspice

¼ teaspoon ground cinnamon

¼ cup packed light brown sugar

1 teaspoon red pepper flakes

¼ teaspoon ground cloves

¼ teaspoon ground cumin

1 teaspoon fine sea salt

1 teaspoon freshly ground black pepper

3 tablespoons canola oil

8 hot dogs, butterflied

2 cups vegetable oil

3 bananas, peeled and sliced crosswise into ¼-inch-thick slices

8 hot dog buns (page 15 or store-bought)

½ cup yellow mustard

1 tablespoon curry paste (sold in the ethnic section of most grocery stores)

(recipe continues)

Mix the allspice, cinnamon, brown sugar, red pepper flakes, cloves, cumin, salt, pepper, and canola oil together in a small bowl. Rub this paste all over the hot dogs, pressing it into the surface. Heat the vegetable oil to 375°F in a large, deep pot.

Fry the bananas until they are lightly browned and crisp, about 3 minutes. Remove the pot from the heat and place the bananas on a paper towel–lined plate to drain.

Meanwhile, heat a skillet over medium-high heat. Add the hot dogs and sear them all over. (The jerk paste will melt and caramelize.) Place the hot dogs in the buns. Mix the mustard and curry paste together in a small bowl and drizzle it on top of the hot dogs.

Top with the fried bananas.

General Tso's Wiener

Every Chinese restaurant in America sells General Tso's chicken—and a lot of it. The spicy, sweet, tangy sauce is addictive. And when it's adorning a hot dog, even better! We deep-fry this dog in an egg roll skin, which gives it awesome crunch.

1 tablespoon vegetable oil

2 garlic cloves, minced

2 tablespoons peeled and freshly grated ginger

1 cup low-sodium chicken broth

⅛ cup low-sodium soy sauce

2 tablespoons orange juice

1 tablespoon cornstarch

1 teaspoon sambal oelek (chile-garlic sauce found in the Asian section of most grocery stores)

3 tablespoons raw or Demerara sugar

4 teaspoons Dijon mustard

8 egg roll wrappers

8 hot dogs

4 cups peanut or vegetable oil (or enough to come 2 inches up the sides of your pot)

2 tablespoons freshly chopped chives

(recipe continues)

Heat the vegetable oil in a medium saucepan over high heat. Add the garlic and ginger and sauté until fragrant, about 30 seconds.

In a separate bowl, mix together the chicken broth, soy sauce, orange juice, cornstarch, sambal oelek, and raw sugar.

Add this mixture to the ginger-garlic mixture and bring to a boil. Stir until the sauce is thick and shiny. Remove the pan from the heat and cover it to keep it warm.

Put ½ teaspoon of mustard in a line down the center of each egg roll wrapper and place a hot dog on top. Roll the wrapper up like an egg roll, tucking the ends in to make a cylindrical package.

Heat the peanut oil to 375°F in a large, deep pot.

Fry the wieners a few at a time until they are brown and crisp, about 2 minutes. Place the cooked wieners on a paper towel–lined plate to cool. When all the hot dogs are fried, pour the sauce over them and sprinkle them with the chives.

Phyllo Fido

A hot dog lover's version of the Greek classic spanakopita. We made this for a guy in our office, and he said, "I don't even eat hot dogs, and I love this!" So, there you go. It's dressed to impress, too, with all those pretty colors and flaky phyllo.

· · ✦ ◆ ✦ · ·

Preheat the oven to 400°F.

Prepare a stack of 10 sheets of phyllo dough, brushed with 4 ounces of the melted butter as directed on the package. Cut the stack in half crosswise, making 2 equal stacks.

Put 1 split hot dog half on each, then repeat so you have 8 stacks.

Evenly divide the spinach, feta, pine nuts, garlic, and scallions among the stacks, placing an even amount on top of each dog half. Sprinkle each serving with oregano and black pepper to taste.

Fold each stack of phyllo into a rectangle, ends first, to seal in the contents. Place each rectangle seam-side down on a cookie sheet and brush each with the reserved 2 tablespoons of melted butter.

Place the phyllo packets on a parchment or foil-lined baking sheet and bake them for 20 minutes or until browned.

1 (1-pound) box frozen phyllo dough (thawed according to package directions)

4 ounces (1 stick) unsalted butter, plus 2 tablespoons, melted

4 hot dogs, butterflied and cut in half crosswise

1 (6-ounce) bag baby spinach

4 ounces feta cheese

4 ounces pine nuts, toasted

2 garlic cloves, minced

1 bunch scallions (white and light green parts only), chopped

1 teaspoon dried oregano

Freshly ground black pepper

Lasagna Dog

The meat is the best part of any lasagna, right? Well, the Lasagna Dog puts it front and center! This recipe comes together pretty quickly and takes about half the time in the oven as regular lasagna. You can use hot or sweet sausage, depending on whether you like it spicy or not, and you can either make your own spaghetti sauce or crack open a jar. Either way, this is a sure crowd-pleaser.

2½ cups spaghetti sauce (recipe follows or store-bought), divided

8 Italian sausage links (hot or sweet)

¾ (15-ounce) container part-skim ricotta cheese

⅓ cup grated Parmesan cheese

⅓ teaspoon fine sea salt

1 garlic clove, minced or crushed through a press

1 large egg

Freshly ground black pepper

Large handful fresh basil, chopped

10 dried lasagna noodles, boiled (a few extra in case a couple break)

2½ cups shredded part-skim mozzarella cheese, divided

Large handful fresh parsley, chopped, for garnish

(recipe continues)

Preheat the oven to 400°F.

Cover the bottom of an 8-inch square casserole dish with ½ cup of spaghetti sauce. Brown the sausages over medium-high heat in a skillet and let them cool.

Combine the ricotta, Parmesan, salt, garlic, egg, pepper, and chopped basil in a small bowl. Lay a noodle flat and spread a spoonful of the ricotta mixture over the top. Sprinkle with ⅛ cup of the mozzarella cheese.

Take 1 sausage link and place it crosswise on the noodle at one end. Roll the sausage tightly in the noodle and place it in the casserole dish. Repeat with the remaining noodles, ricotta mixture, and sausages.

Pour the remaining spaghetti sauce over the roll-ups and sprinkle with the remaining mozzarella cheese. Cover the pan tightly with aluminum foil.

Bake the lasagna for 20 minutes. Remove the foil and bake for an additional 5 minutes until the sauce is bubbly and the cheese is browned. Sprinkle some parsley on top for garnish.

SPAGHETTI SAUCE

MAKES ABOUT 7 CUPS

Heat the olive oil over medium heat and add the garlic. Sizzle the garlic for a few seconds to soften it, and then add the tomatoes and red wine. Stir the mixture and bring it to a simmer. Simmer the sauce over low heat for 30 minutes to blend the flavors. Add the red pepper flakes, sugar, basil, and salt and pepper to taste. Taste and correct the seasonings if necessary. Store the sauce in an airtight container in the refrigerator for up to 1 week, or freeze it for up to 2 months.

3 tablespoons olive oil

4 garlic cloves, minced or crushed through a press

3 (28-ounce) cans crushed tomatoes

1 cup dry red wine

¼ teaspoon red pepper flakes

1 teaspoon granulated sugar

Large handful fresh basil, thinly sliced

Salt and freshly ground black pepper

Formulas for
Metric Conversions

FORMULAS FOR METRIC CONVERSION

•••••••••••••••••••••••••••••••••••••

Ounces to grams
multiply ounces by 28.35

Cups to liters
multiply cups by .24

METRIC EQUIVALENTS FOR WEIGHT

•••••••••••••••••••••••••••••••••••••

U.S.	Metric
1 oz	28 g
2 oz	57 g
3 oz	85 g
4 oz	113 g
5 oz	142 g
6 oz	170 g
7 oz	198 g
8 oz	227 g
16 oz (1 lb.)	454 g
2.2 lbs.	1 kg

METRIC EQUIVALENTS FOR VOLUME

•••••••••••••••••••••••••••••••••••••

U.S.	Metric	
⅛ tsp.	0.6 ml	—
¼ tsp.	1.2 ml	—
½ tsp.	2.5 ml	—
¾ tsp.	3.7 ml	—
1 tsp.	5 ml	—
1½ tsp.	7.4 ml	—
2 tsp.	10 ml	—
1 Tbsp.	15 ml	—
1½ Tbsp.	22 ml	—
2 Tbsp. (⅛ cup)	30 ml	1 fl. oz
3 Tbsp.	45 ml	—
¼ cup	59 ml	2 fl. oz
⅓ cup	79 ml	—
½ cup	118 ml	4 fl. oz
⅔ cup	58 ml	—
¾ cup	178 ml	6 fl. oz
1 cup	237 ml	8 fl. oz
1¼ cups	300 ml	—
1½ cups	355 ml	—
1¾ cups	425 ml	—
2 cups (1 pint)	500 ml	16 fl. oz
3 cups	725 ml	—
4 cups (1 quart)	.95 liters	32 fl. oz
16 cups (1 gallon)	3.8 liters	128 fl. oz

Acknowledgments

This book was born in a hotel bar in Dallas, Texas, where we were traveling on business. We love to cook, create, and eat hot dogs, but we were astonished to find that there was not a cookbook of creative hot dog recipes out there. So, we started brainstorming different ideas for hot dog recipes. That list eventually became *Wieners Gone Wild!,* and we have Jordana Tusman and Chris Navratil at Running Press to thank for believing in the concept and in our ability to pull it off, and Zac Leibman for pushing it across the finish line. Special thanks to designer Jason Kayser for his skill and patience. We couldn't have found a better home, or more talented people to usher our brainchild into the world.

Thank you to our team at Hollan Publishing, especially Becky Tarr Thomas and Monica Sweeney, who kept the business running smoothly while we were cooking and shooting, and Dalyn Miller, whose creativity and passion for food is an inspiration. And to all the authors we've worked with over the years—we now know firsthand how hard you work to bring our ideas to life!

HOLLY

Enormous thanks to: My parents, in-laws, and extended family, who are always enthusiastic about my business endeavors, especially when they're amusing; my friends in Hamilton-Wenham, who have made suburban parenthood infinitely more fun; Bruce Lubin, for helping me navigate this crazy business, and a lot else; Kara and Shaun Sparks, for the hot dog bun pan and twenty years of friendship; and, of course, my husband, Michael, and our children, who let me think I'm in charge and fill my life with joy. Finally, to my business partner and co-author, Allan Penn, for your talent, courage, loyalty, and unparalleled sense of humor—there is nobody I'd rather throw knives at.

ALLAN

First, I'd like to thank Oscar Mayer, without whom none of this would have been possible. To my mom and dad, thanks for the nitrites. Childhood would not have been the same without them. To my three sisters, thanks for believing that someday I would amount to something, even though this probably wasn't what you had in mind. To my wife, Lisa, and our children, you inspire me even more than General Tso's Wiener— and that's saying something. To one of the funniest, most talented, and creative people I know, my co-author, Holly Schmidt: rice to the paella!

Index

B

BACON

BARBECUE

BEEF *See also* Sausage

BREADS, BISCUITS, & PANCAKES

BREAKFAST & BRUNCH

SOUPS & STEWS

T

TOPPINGS. *See* Condiments, Relishes, Salsas & Sauces

TORTILLAS